1987: The first animated GIF is created.

1991: Scientists at Cambridge University track coffee levels using the first webcam. By 1993, everyone on the internet can tune in.

1996: Andrew Weinreich founds the first social networking site, SixDegrees.

1999: Kevin Ashton comes up with the idea for the Internet of Things.

2001: The first phones with Bluetooth are released.

Curious?
Turn the page!

active★minds

BOOK of FIRSTS

First to the Future

HOW was artificial intelligence first used?

WHEN was the first webcam invented?

WHO is the youngest computer programmer?

Inventors, Innovators, and Ideas

Written by
Dale Jones

sequoia kids media
An imprint of PHOENIX International Publications, Inc.

Visit us at
SequoiaKidsMedia.com
for bonus downloadable content

Art © Shutterstock 2024 ghenadie; Borisovna.art; Shmer; Click Bestsellers; chinasong; tynyuk; FeelGoodLuck; ledokolua; Wise ant; zentilia; Vasyl Nagernyak; tovovan; Albert Garridol; the8monkey; stockphoto-graf; cobalt88; Hilch; RSplaneta; Katt_Polyakova; Faber14; Vectorfair; bsd studio; Prostock-studio; John B Hewitt; Prachaya Roekdeethaweesab; Mozaic Studio; vectorisland; Marta Sher; Milles Vector Studio; Sandra_M; rizki dian pratama; Kaissa; Mironov Konstantin; James Copeland; ANITA'S Studio; picturepixx; Nikelser Kate; Intellson; Creative Stall; Elena Pimukova; 300 librarians; metamorworks; cristi180884; lucadp; NazArt; Wanderlust Media; Room27; fizkes; aleksandr_pa_vector; Antikwar; veronawinner; Dzm1try; Elfangor; beautifullyhit; Janos Levente; Balora; Aozora21; Victoruler; Kjpargeter; magicinfoto; Overearth; Arcady; Supza; Ayunannas; bysho; pingebat; Boule; Maciej Es; a-image; olesia_g; KsanaGraphica; TechSolution; yaistantine; indahp; Sk Hasan Ali; WinWin artlab; bymandesigns; Design Ful; University of College; krissikunterbunt; solarus; GaluhSekar; Digital Vector Media; Eightshot_Studio; r.classen
© Wikimedia Commons 2024 Ståle Grut/NRKbeta (pg 7); tara hunt (pg 10); NEXT Conference (pg 13); Pmox (pg 15); RLCRoet (pg 18); Skarr21 (pg 18); Larry D. Moore (pg 19); UNCTAD (pg 20); Taelim8774 (pg 22); © Flickr 2024 cellanr (pg 12); R.Farrell/ITU Pictures (pg 21); © Freepik 2024 Darius Dan (pg 18)

Published by Sequoia Kids Media,
an imprint of Sequoia Publishing & Media, LLC

Sequoia Publishing & Media, LLC,
a division of Phoenix International Publications, Inc.

8501 West Higgins Road, Chicago, Illinois 60631
34 Seymour Street, London W1H 7JE
Heimhuder Straße 81, 20148 Hamburg

CustomerService@PhoenixInternational.com

www.SequoiaKidsMedia.com

Library of Congress Control Number: 2024933043

ISBN: 979-8-7654-0720-2

Table of Contents

Introduction

The world today looks very different from the world 200 years ago. But it's also much different than it was 20 years ago! The evolution of technology has changed the way people work, behave, and even think. Some inventions make it easier to manufacture goods that people can buy in stores. And some can't even be seen!

The internet is invisible, but billions of people use it every day. People use Bluetooth to listen to music. They talk to digital assistants like Amazon's Alexa and Apple's Siri.

Thanks to the internet, the world is more connected than ever. Devices can even talk to each other! They can tell when something is broken or adjust the temperature in your house. Every year, there are new inventions. People are coming up with ideas all the time!

Technology You Use Every Day

- Microwaves
- Cars
- Cell phones
- Computers
- Tablets
- And so much more!

Christopher Strachey

November 16, 1916–May 18, 1975

Wrote the first AI computer game

Christopher Strachey didn't start programming computers until he was 34 years old. He wanted to write a **computer program** that could play checkers. The computer could use an early type of AI to look ahead and figure out moves. He finished the program in 1951. But when he ran it, the computer's memory filled up too fast. This made the game crash. He needed to find a better computer.

He talked to his friend **Alan Turing**. Turing agreed to let him use a different computer at Manchester University. This computer was much more powerful. By the summer of 1952, Strachey's program could play a complete game of checkers.

AI stands for **"artificial intelligence."** That's a machine's ability to mimic a human brain. AI can look at its surroundings, make decisions, and learn.

Strachey and Turing worked together later. They made a program that could write **love letters**. It used about 70 base words but reordered them so no note was ever the same.

Now, many video games use AI. AI characters in games react based on what the human players do.

Kimberly Bryant

January 14, 1967–present

Founded Black Girls Code, the first coding program for minorities in the Bay Area

Kimberly Bryant lived in Silicon Valley, a global center for computer and technology development. Her daughter wanted to learn **how to code**. She went to a summer camp. But there weren't many girls there. And there were no other Black girls.

Bryant didn't think that this was right. She wanted her daughter to succeed. In 2011, she founded **Black Girls Code**. Black Girls Code encourages young Black girls to get involved in computer programming. It also teaches web design and robotics.

Now, it teaches girls all over the United States. There is even a program in South Africa! Within the first three years, 3,000 girls learned to code from the organization.

Only **22 percent** of all programmers are women. Only **5 percent** of all programmers are Black. But both those numbers are growing as minorities in coding become more accepted.

When people learn to code, they're not just learning to make programs. They also learn **logical thinking, teamwork, creativity, and analytical skills**. Learning to code also helps kids in the future. Technology-related jobs are growing and can be found in every field. Doctors, teachers, construction workers, and even agricultural workers use new tech.

William Tunstall-Pedoe

January 29, 1969–present

Wrote code that became Alexa, the first popular smart speaker

In 2005, **William Tunstall-Pedoe** founded a company called **True Knowledge**. In 2012, he released an app called Evi. It used advanced AI to help users get answers! Other companies were impressed.

One of these companies was Amazon. Amazon bought Tunstall-Pedoe's company for $26 million. They used it to create a digital assistant called **Alexa**. Alexa launched in 2014.

By 2016, it knew 135 skills. Amazon encouraged everyday people to teach Alexa new skills. Soon, Alexa was solving math problems, summarizing the news, and even playing fart noises.

By 2020, it had learned more than **100,000 skills**. Now, Alexa comes built into all Amazon Echo devices.

Alexa wasn't the very first voice-activated tech. But it kickstarted the smart speaker trend.

Some top Alexa skills include:

- Easy Yoga
- Brain Workout
- Roast Me
- Sleep Sounds
- Uwu Voice

Kautilya Katariya

2013–present

First six-year-old computer programmer

When **Kautilya Katariya** was five years old, his father bought him a book about **computer programming**. He read the whole book in one day. Then, he started coding.

When he was six, Katariya set a **Guinness World Record**. He was the youngest Python programmer ever. Python is a computer programming language.

By age nine, Katariya was already taking high school math classes. He also did university programming competitions.

Katariya started taking lessons online from IBM. He also took classes from Stanford University, Microsoft, and MIT.

In 2023, he started **TheDeciphers**. It is a place for young problem-solvers to meet and chat.

Katariya wrote a program that plays tic-tac-toe.

People hire Katariya to speak at computer programming conferences.

Katariya loves origami, biking, and swimming.

Katariya hopes to someday develop a new AI.

Dr. Quentin Stafford-Fraser and Dr. Paul Jardetzky

Created the first intranet webcam

At a **computer science lab** at Cambridge University in England, there was one important piece of equipment. It was the coffeepot! It was kept in a lab called the Trojan Room.

Scientists were always disappointed when they found the pot empty. Two of them were **Dr. Quentin Stafford-Fraser and Dr. Paul Jardetzky**. In 1991, they pointed a camera at the pot. Then, they wrote some code.

The code told the camera to **take a picture** three times a minute. The pictures were saved on the internal network. People at Cambridge could check if the pot was empty or full without leaving their workspace.

Dr. Quentin Stafford-Fraser

Dr. Martyn Johnson

Created the first internet webcam

On November 22, 1993, **Dr. Martyn Johnson** was working in the lab. The camera was still working, but he wasn't connected to the internal network. He wrote some code that put the pictures on the internet instead. He'd made the **world's first webcam**.

Once it was on the internet, everyone could see it. People all over the world started checking on the coffeepot. Some even asked if a light could be left on overnight so it could be seen no matter what time it was! Some people visited the lab just to see the coffeepot in person.

An intranet is a private network. Only people part of a group or organization can access it. The internet is open to anyone.

After streaming 10,000 brewed pots, the webcam and the coffeepot were finally turned off in August 2001. Newspapers all over the world wrote articles about it.

The coffeepot was sold online for £3,350. That's around $4,800!

Today, people can tune into webcams around the world–and beyond! Watching eagle eggs hatch or penguins waddle by is something thousands of people tune in to see.

Andrew Weinreich

Created the first social networking site

In May 1996, **Andrew Weinreich** founded the first social networking site for adults. Eventually, it would be called **SixDegrees**.

People could make a **profile** and add **real-life friends**. They could also meet new people based on their interests. It was the first site to blend all these features.

In 1999, Weinreich sold his website. SixDegrees doesn't exist today, but it set the stage for all the **social networking sites** that we use today, like Facebook, Instagram, and X, formerly known as Twitter.

SixDegrees was named after the Six Degrees of Separation Theory. It says that we are connected by six "degrees" to everyone else on the planet.

A "degree" is one connection. You and your friend have one degree of separation. If your friend has a cousin that you don't know, that's two degrees of separation.

Not many people had access to the internet at the time. But at its height, more than 3.5 million people were registered on SixDegrees.

Chris Messina

Posted the first hashtag on X

When X first started, it was hard for people to search for or follow a topic. It also couldn't track trending topics.

BarCamp is a way to hold a meeting. There is no leader or speaker. The participants all contribute.

Chris Messina wanted to change that. On August 23, 2007, Messina posted the first **hashtag**, #barcamp, to Twitter. The # sign would make it easy to search for keywords rather than whole discussions. At first, nobody else used hashtags.

How do you feel about using # (pound) for groups. As in #barcamp [msg]?

–@chrismessina, Twitter, August 23, 2007

Now, more than 125 million hashtags are shared on X every day. Other social media sites use them too. X even celebrates August 23 as #HashtagDay.

But then, in October, a wildfire broke out in San Diego. Chris encouraged a friend in San Diego to try using #sandiegowildfire. People started using the hashtag to discuss what was going on.

The **pound symbol** is also called the number symbol, or hash. That's how it became known as a hashtag. People were using the hash (#) to tag topics so they could be found.

Marie Van Brittan Brown

October 30, 1922–February 2, 1999

Designed the first home security system

Marie Van Brittan Brown worked as a nurse in New York City. Her husband was an electronics technician. They both worked long hours. They lived in a **high-crime neighborhood**. Sometimes, Brown came home very late at night. She worried about her safety.

Brown and her husband worked on a **home security system** to help them feel safe. They thought it was so good that they applied for a patent. It was granted in 1969. Their system used several peepholes and two-way microphones. There was also a camera and television monitors. Brown could see who was outside. She could talk to them from inside her home. There was also an **emergency button**. If she pressed it, the police would get an alert and come to help.

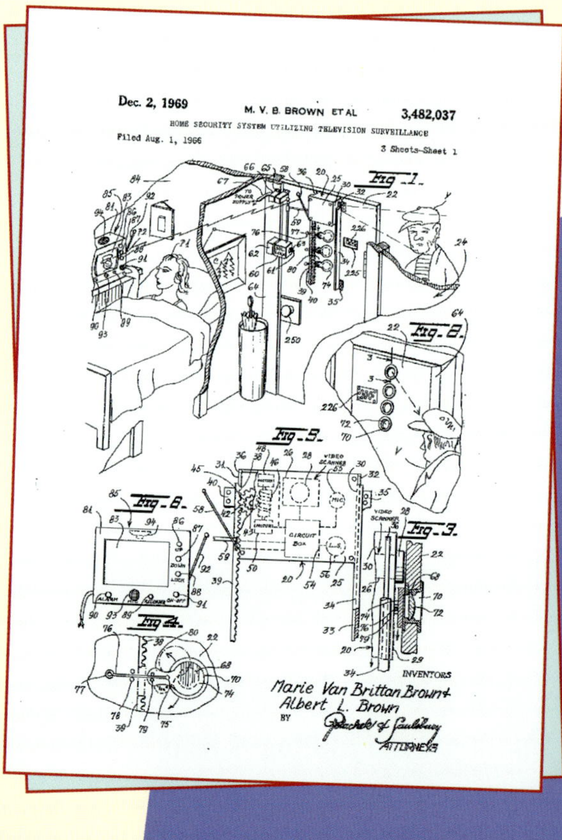

People started to notice what she'd done. The ***New York Times*** interviewed her. Her patent was referenced by many other people. It was the start of a new era in home security.

Patents give creators rights to how their invention is made or used. Patents are granted for all sorts of inventions! In 2022, more than 278,000 international patents were filed.

History of Home Security

Ancient people didn't have cameras and phones. They had to find other ways to protect themselves. They built their homes on top of hills so they could see if anyone was coming. Later, they dug moats and built drawbridges. Dogs barked if they saw strangers.

Benjamin Franklin used his own version of home security. It wasn't high-tech. It was just three mirrors attached to a window. The mirrors let him see who was at the front door without being seen himself. He didn't just use them for safety. He also used them to avoid people he didn't want to talk to!

Memeworthy

The first memes, GIFs, and more

Richard Dawkins came up with the word **meme** back in 1976. It comes from the Greek word for "imitated." But humans have used memes for all of recorded history. A meme is really just an idea that everyone is familiar with. It can be used to quickly convey information. And it can change and evolve at a moment's notice.

This meme from 1921 is shockingly similar to memes today!

The first animated **GIF** showed up on the internet in 1987. Engineer **Stephen Wilhite** worked for an internet company called CompuServe. He created a GIF of an airplane. Clouds in the background moved in a loop.

The word *GIF* stands for Graphics Interchange Format.

GIF or JIF?

Wilhite says *GIF* is pronounced with a *j* sound. But some argue that graphics starts with the letter *g*, and so it should be pronounced with a hard *g* sound.

In 1996, a software company called Autodesk released a program called 3D Studio Max. It was used to create **3D models** and **animation**. It gave users examples of how to use the software.

One of these examples was a short video of a **dancing baby**. A software developer named John Woodell turned it into a GIF. He started emailing it to people. People made edits of it. They posted these online. TV shows even used it in stories! This was one of the first internet memes.

In 2006, web developer **Alex King** invented the first **Share** button. Its symbol was three connected dots. Before, people had to copy and paste text into a new document. Now, they could share stories, funny cat videos, and posts with the click of a button. Other people copied his idea. They use different icons, but the idea is still the same.

Jaap Haartsen

February 13, 1963–present

Invented Bluetooth

In 1994, **Jaap Haartsen** worked for a Swedish company called Ericsson. The company wanted a way for electronic devices to **connect** to each other **without wires**. Haartsen had an answer. He thought of a system that would let devices communicate when they were close together through radio waves.

He named his invention **Bluetooth**. In 2001, the first phones with Bluetooth were released. Now, almost all electronics come with it.

Bluetooth is named after an ancient king. He united Denmark and Norway, like Haartsen's invention united devices. He was famous for a dead tooth. People gave him the nickname "Bluetooth."

People use Bluetooth to **listen to music** and **make phone calls**. It can also be used to play video games with friends or send pictures. Bluetooth tracks temperature and connects home security. It's used all over the world, for all sorts of things!

Kevin Ashton

Invented the first standardized RFID technology and the Internet of Things

The first computers got all their information from humans. There weren't any automatic sensors or detectors. The computers weren't directly connected to the world.

In 1999, **Kevin Ashton** dreamed of a world where computers were connected. Sensors would monitor objects and talk to each other. He called it the **"Internet of Things,"** or **IoT**.

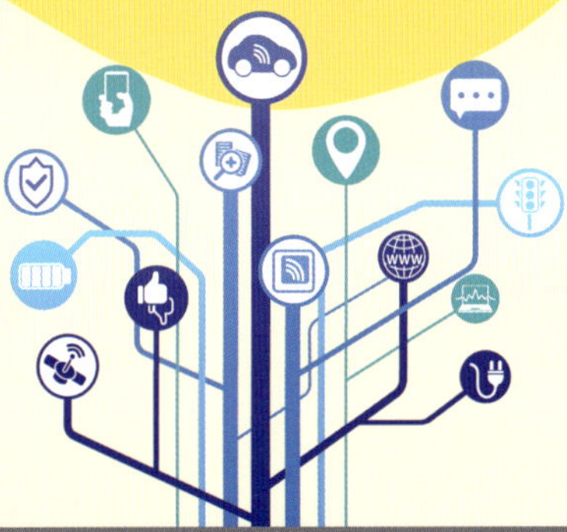

Ashton founded the Auto-ID Laboratory at MIT. It helped standardize **RFID technology**. That's short for radio-frequency identification. The wireless technology lets readers identify and track tags inside everyday objects.

Credit card machines with tap technology use RFID. So do no-swipe ticket passes at amusement parks. Packages can be tracked from the moment they leave the warehouse to when they're dropped off at your front door.

By 2023, more than **15 billion** devices were connected. Kitchen appliances, cars, TVs, smart light bulbs, robots, and even traffic lights are linked up through the IoT!

In 2014, NASA launched **Project RFID**. Tracking equipment and monitoring spacecraft in outer space can make astronauts' jobs easier and safer.

Sophia

February 14, 2016–present

First advanced humanlike robot

For years, **David Hanson** worked as a **Disney Imagineer**. He helped design and build theme parks and attractions. But he wanted to go beyond that. He wanted to build a robot that looked and sounded like a person. His company, Hanson Robotics, was founded in 2005.

In February of 2016, the company finally made this robot. **Sophia** can make more than **60 facial expressions**. Her eyes and chest have cameras that help her see.

The AI she uses helps her remember faces and talk to people. She can do research and teach people what she has learned. Hanson Robotics says she even has her own emotions. A combination of AI, speech recognition tech, and computer vision helps her **learn and improve**.

Sophia has appeared on **TV shows**. She gives talks at conferences all over the world.

Sophia can move her hands, eyes, and body. She can walk on legs or roll on wheels attached to a tripod-shaped base.

In 2017, Saudi Arabia granted Sophia citizenship. She became the first **nonhuman citizen** of any country. Sophia also has a passport.

The United Nations Development Program made her the first robot **Innovation Ambassador**.

Hanson Robotics also makes and sells a **Little Sophia**. She is 14 inches (35.6 centimeters) tall. She can talk and sing. Kids can learn about STEM, coding, and AI from Little Sophia. They can program her by using the coding languages Blockly and Python.

Charles "Chuck" Hull

May 12, 1939–present

Invented the first commercial 3D printer

In the 1980s, **Charles Hull** was working for a company that used **UV lamps**. The lamps hardened a thin layer of a material called veneer onto objects.

Hull had an idea. He wondered if UV lamps could be used to print objects made out of a type of plastic called resin.

He started experimenting. By 1986, Hull had a patent for an SLA 3D printer. It was the first commercial 3D printing technology.

3D printers expose **liquid resin** to a UV light. The resin hardens in a pattern. A 3D object is built using many, many layers of that resin.

Anything You Can Imagine

Today, there are a lot of different 3D printers. Some are used to test **new medicines**. Others are used in construction. They can print using concrete. Construction sites make less waste that way. Now, **whole houses** can be 3D printed! Anything you can imagine can be 3D printed.

Ms. Tang Yu

August 26, 2022–present

First virtual AI robot CEO

NetDragon Websoft is a software company that makes online video games and mobile apps. In August 2022, the company announced that it had a **new CEO**. Her name is **Ms. Tang Yu**. But this CEO isn't a person. She is AI!

Ms. Tang Yu was the first AI CEO in the world. She does all the things a human CEO would do. She signs documents and assigns tasks. She makes decisions for the company. NetDragon said she would make the company more efficient and organized.

Many people doubted Ms. Tang Yu. But in her first six months, NetDragon's value jumped to over a **billion dollars**.

Extra Firsts!

The first use of the word *robot* dates back to 1920.

The pound symbol was first used centuries ago! Many believe it comes from the Latin phrase *libra pondo,* which means "pound of weight."

In September 2022, an AI robot named Mika was named the first humanoid CEO. She is a life-size robot that uses AI.

Read More

Bolte, Mari. *How the Internet Will Save the World.* Fremont, CA: Full Tilt Press, 2023.

Hadlett, Gaelen. *Exploring AI.* North Mankato, MN: Capstone Press, 2024.

Schwartz, Heather E. *Edge of Medicine: Medical Artificial Intelligence Breakthroughs.* Rochester, MN: Mayo Clinic Press, 2023.

2006: Alex King invents the first Share button.

2007: Chris Messina posts the first hashtag.

2011: Kimberly Bryant founds Black Girls Code, the first coding program for minorities in the Bay Area.

2012: William Tunstall-Pedoe releases Evi, an app that paves the way for the smart speaker Alexa.

2016: Sophia, the first advanced humanlike robot, is released by Hanson Robotics.